Christmas story-book box

Glue

Glue

Glue

Glue

Cut out box.
Score dotted lines.
Glue flaps and fold
up box, sticking
flaps inside.

Cut out and glue
story strip together.
Score and fold.
Glue flap inside
bottom of box.

Glue to bottom of box inside.

Glue to make one long story strip.

Christmas card wreath

Cut slits. Push corners of cards
through and secure with sticky tape at back.

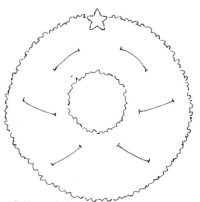 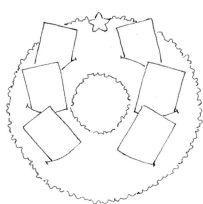

Other ideas for card display.
String and decorated pegs

Ribbon

Stapled

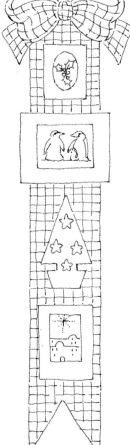

Stack

 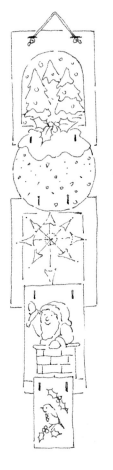

SHEET 3

Glue

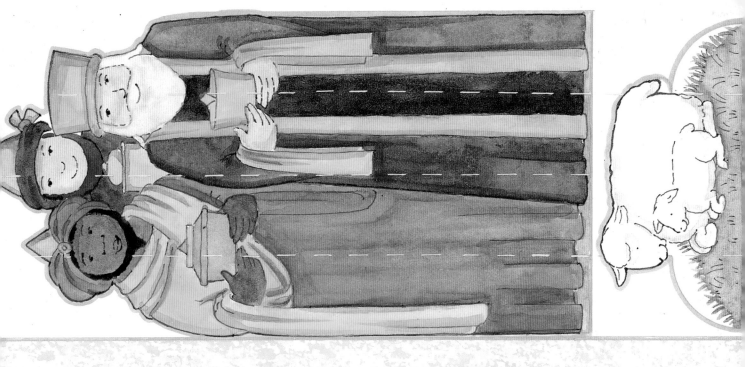

Glue

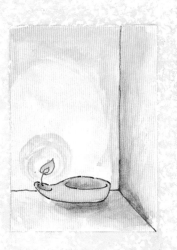

Glue